TRIBES of NATIVE AMERICA

edited by Marla Felkins Ryan
and Linda Schmittroth

BLACKBIRCH®
PRESS

THOMSON

GALE

22228

San Diego • Detroit • New York • San Francisco • Cleveland
New Haven, Conn. • Waterville, Maine • London • Munich

THOMSON

GALE

For more information, contact
The Gale Group, Inc.
27500 Drake Rd.
Farmington Hills, MI 48331-3535
Or you can visit our Internet site at http://www.gale.com

Photo credits: Cover Courtesy of Northwestern University Library; cover © National Archives;
cover © Photospin; cover © Perry Jasper Photography; cover © Picturequest; cover © Seattle
Post-Intelligencer Collection, Museum of History & Industry; cover © PhotoDisc; cover © Library
of Congress; pages 5, 20, 22, 23, 24, 29 (top) © Marilyn "Angel" Wynn, nativestock.com; page 6
© Corel Corporation; pages 7, 18, 25 © Linday Hebberd/CORBIS; pages 8, 10 © North Wind
Picture Archives; pages 11, 28, 30 (both) Courtesy of National Archives; page 12 Courtesy of
Library of Congress; page 14 Courtesy of the Oklahoma Historical Society, #20637, pub. by E.C.
Kropp, Milwaukee, WI; pages 15, 21 © Stapleton Collection/CORBIS; pages 17, 20 © Smithsonian
American Art Museum, Washington, D.C./Art Resource, N.Y.; page 19 Courtesy of Western
History Collections, University of Oklahoma Library; page 29 (bottom) © Hulton Archives

LIBRARY OF CONGRESS CATALOGING-IN-PUBLICATION DATA

Kiowa / Marla Felkins Ryan, book editor ; Linda Schmittroth, book editor.
   v. cm. — (Tribes of Native America)
Includes bibliographical references and index.
Contents: Name — History — Government — Daily life — Current tribal issues.
  ISBN 1-56711-692-2 (alk. paper)
  1. Kiowa Indians—History—Juvenile literature. 2. Kiowa Indians—Social life and
customs—Juvenile literature. [1. Kiowa Indians. 2. Indians of North America—Great
Plains.] I. Ryan, Marla Felkins. II. Schmittroth, Linda. III. Series.

  E99.K5K56 2003
  978.004'9749—dc21

               2003002629

Printed in United States
10 9 8 7 6 5 4 3 2 1

Table of Contents

KIOWA

Name

Kiowa (pronounced *KIE-uh-wuh*). The name comes
from the Comanche word *Kaigwa,* which means "two
halves differ." The word described the Kiowa
warriors' hairstyle. Warriors cut their hair on only
one side and left the other side long. Over time, the
name changed into Kiowa. The name Kiowa means
"the principal people."

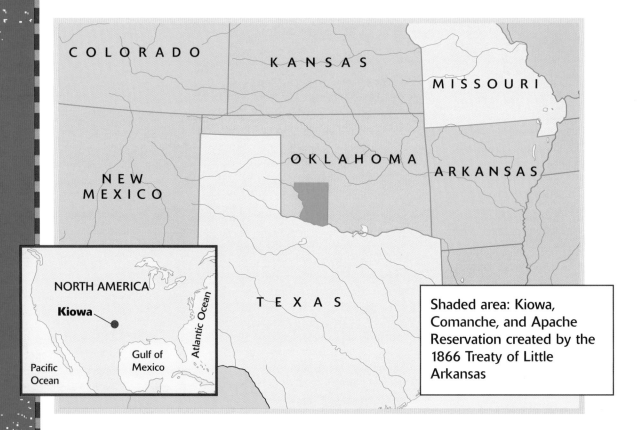

Shaded area: Kiowa,
Comanche, and Apache
Reservation created by the
1866 Treaty of Little
Arkansas

This modern-day Kiowa man's ceremonial dress links him to the traditions of his cultural past.

Where are the traditional Kiowa lands?

The Kiowa first lived in parts of present-day Montana. In 1700, they lived near the Black Hills of South Dakota. The Kiowa moved to the southwestern Great Plains in 1785. In the 1990s, about sixty-five hundred Kiowa lived in small cities in southwest Oklahoma. They lived near the spot where their old reservation used to be.

The Kiowa first settled near the Yellowstone River (pictured above) in what is now southwest Montana.

What has happened to the population?

In the early nineteenth century, there were about eighteen hundred Kiowa. In a 1990 population count by the U.S. Census Bureau, 9,460 people said they were Kiowa.

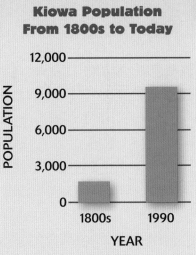

Kiowa Population From 1800s to Today

POPULATION

12,000

9,000

6,000

3,000

0

1800s   1990

YEAR

Origins and group ties

Tribal stories say the Kiowa first lived in western Montana. They made their home near the sources of the Missouri and Yellowstone Rivers. The Kiowa say their ancestors came into this world from an underworld. Their ancestors had to go through a hollow log between the two worlds. On the way out, a pregnant woman became stuck. She blocked the way so those behind her could not get out. This is why there were so few Kiowa. Some Kiowa married Sarci Indians and created a tribe called the Kiowa Apache. After 1700, the Kiowa were alternately friends and enemies with the Apache, Crow, and Cheyenne.

Although they were few in number, the Kiowa were respected as fierce warriors. Their violent battles against American settlement of their homeland made them legends.

Kiowa at a powwow dance celebrate the warrior spirit of their ancestors. The Kiowa, along with the Comanche, were known as the fiercest warriors of the Great Plains.

HISTORY

Early days on the Great Plains

The ancient Kiowa were hunters. They wandered the Great Plains as they followed the vast herds of buffalo. The buffalo was the tribe's main food source. In the seventeenth century, French explorer René-Robert Cavelier was the first European to write about the Kiowa. He did not meet the tribe face-to-face, but he wrote that the Kiowa owned many horses. The tribe probably got their horses from Spanish settlers in Mexico.

By the 1700s, the Kiowa had roamed as far east as the Black Hills of South Dakota. There, the tiny tribe became friends with the large and powerful Crow nation. To gain honor in their tribes, Plains Indians led raids, stole

René-Robert Cavelier was the first European explorer to write about the Kiowa.

horses, and waged war. They fought with the Comanche and Shoshone in the west, the Cheyenne and Arapaho in the north, and the Sioux in the east. The Crow and Kiowa lived well from their lifestyle.

Move to southern Plains

In 1781, a smallpox outbreak killed nearly two thousand Kiowa. Worn down by illness and the constant battles, the Kiowa decided to leave the Black Hills area. In 1785, the tribe moved to the southern Plains. Soon afterward, the weakened Kiowa made peace with the much larger Comanche tribe. The two tribes agreed to share hunting grounds. Often, Kiowa and Comanche joined forces in raids against other tribes. Together, they took control of the southern Plains from the Apache and Wichita. They gained a reputation as the fiercest of Plains warriors, especially in Texas and New Mexico. They met Spanish settlers in those states and began to trade with them. The two tribes also began to attack white settlements.

American explorers Meriwether Lewis and William Clark met the Kiowa in 1804. The Kiowa had just begun to trade with the French. At a French trading post, Lewis and Clark watched the Kiowa sing and dance at a large trade fair.

1869
Transcontinential Railroad is completed

1901–1906
Kiowa-Comanche reservation is broken up into allotments and opened for white settlement

1917–1918
WWI fought in Europe

1929
Stock market crash begins the Great Depression

1941
Bombing at Pearl Harbor forces United States into WWII

1945
WWII ends

1950s
Reservations no longer controlled by federal government

1989–1990
The National Museum of the American Indian Act and the Native American Grave Protection and Reparations Act bring about the return of burial remains to native tribes

Warriors from different Native American tribes worked together to attack white settlers' wagon trains.

Disasters strike

Smallpox outbreaks struck in 1801 and 1816. Many Plains Indians died from the diseases brought by white settlers. Although weak, the Kiowa continued their fights and raids. Soon, great numbers of white settlers began to move across the Great Plains. Most tribes joined forces to attack the wagon trains. This teamwork did not include the Osage. In 1833, Osage warriors had attacked a group of Kiowa as they gathered food. Many Kiowa were killed and beheaded in what was called the Cut-Throat Massacre. Some Kiowa women and children were taken captive.

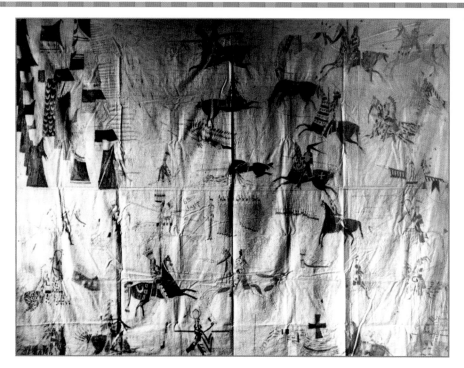

This Kiowa painting shows a battle between the Kiowa and Osage. Osage warriors killed many Kiowa in the Cut-Throat Massacre.

In 1834, U.S. soldiers returned one captive girl taken in the massacre to the Kiowa. This peaceful act was the first meeting between the U.S. government and the Kiowa. The government wanted to end warfare on the Plains and open the area for white settlement. The Kiowa agreed to listen.

In 1837, the Kiowa signed their first treaty with the United States. The Treaty of Fort Gibson gave U.S. citizens the right to travel freely through Indian lands. The Kiowa were given hunting rights in the southern Plains. This area included land that later became the state of Texas. Two years later, another smallpox outbreak swept through the Plains. In 1849, half the tribe died from a cholera outbreak.

More treaties

The Kiowa strongly objected as settlers moved into Texas. The tribe continued to lead raids there. When Texas became a state in 1845, the U.S. government stepped in to end the troubles in the region. When the U.S. Army could not stop the Kiowa, a government agent was sent to talk peace. In 1853, he convinced the Kiowa to sign the Treaty of Fort Atkinson. The treaty called for peace in the region. It also gave the Kiowa money to let the U.S. government build roads and forts without the fear of attacks.

Kiowa and Comanche warriors continued their raids against Indians and whites alike. Finally, the U.S. government called for a new peace council in 1865. The result was the Treaty of Little Arkansas. The treaty called for the Kiowa to move onto a reservation with the Comanche and the Kiowa

The U.S. government arranged peace councils like this one at Medicine Creek, Kansas, with the Kiowa and other tribes to end their attacks on settlers and each other.

Apache. The reservation was in Indian Territory (present-day Oklahoma). The tribes would be forced to give up their other lands. When the tribes refused to sign the treaty, the government agreed to allow them to hunt in western Kansas and Texas. They still had to make the reservation their home.

Another treaty in 1867 promised cattle, farming equipment, and clothing to the Kiowa if they agreed to learn to farm.

Resistance to farming

The U.S. government wanted to change the warlike Kiowa into peaceful farmers. The idea was make the Indians more like European Americans. The Kiowa resisted this plan. With the Comanche, they continued to raid other tribes and Texans. They were finally stopped by the U.S. military in the winter of 1868 to 1869. General George Armstrong Custer (1839–1876) told the Kiowa that they must surrender or be destroyed.

For the next sixty years, the government tried to make the Kiowa give up their tribal customs. Meanwhile, nearby ranchers and farmers wanted Kiowa land. They asked the government to allow settlement on it. Some sent their cattle there to graze illegally. Bolder men built a railroad on reservation land. Towns soon grew up along the tracks.

The stampede of white settlers to Oklahoma forced the Kiowa from their reservations onto even smaller plots of land.

In 1887, Congress passed the General Allotment Act. The act called for the break up of reservation lands into small plots called allotments. Any land that was left over would be sold to whites.

Reservation lost

The Kiowa did not like the idea of allotments. The tribe filed lawsuits, but they could not overturn the law. In 1901, their land was broken up into small plots. By 1906, each Kiowa had a 160-acre plot of land. The tribe had no reservation to call its own. For years, the Kiowa were very poor. Some Kiowa left for good. Today, some Kiowa live on land in Oklahoma that was once part of the reservation.

Religion

The Kiowa believed in supernatural forces that could give power to human beings. One of the most important spirit forces was the Sun. The Kiowa worshiped the Sun in a ceremony called the Sun Dance.

By 1890, many Kiowa and other Indians were fed up with reservation life. They began to follow the Ghost Dance religion. This religion was started by a Paiute Indian named Wovoka. He told Native Americans to dance until the white man was gone. At that time, the buffalo would be plentiful again. The U.S. government outlawed the Ghost Dance. In 1887, the Kiowa performed their last Ghost Dance.

In the late nineteenth century, many Kiowa began to follow the Peyote (pronounced *pay-OH-tee*) religion. In the ceremony, a person ate some of the peyote cactus. He then entered a trance and saw visions. The Kiowa practiced the Little Moon peyote ceremony, which lasted for one full day.

This painting shows some of the ceremonies of the Sun Dance and the Peyote religion. The Kiowa practiced both.

KIOWA WORDS

The Kiowa language has caught up with modern life. For example, the Kiowa word for automobile, *awdlemodlbidl*, is formed from the words *gyesadl* ("it is hot"), *hodl* ("to kill"), and *kawndedl* ("badly"). The word means "bad, hot killing machine."

Government

Each Kiowa band was ruled by a chief. He was chosen for his religious powers or for his skills as a warrior or healer. Sometimes, all the band chiefs came together to talk about things that were important to the whole tribe. Together, they decided whether to make war or peace with another tribe.

On the reservations, the Kiowa were no longer hunters or warriors. Kiowa men had no chance to gain honor as leaders. The people had to obey government rules.

In the 1930s, new laws were passed that gave tribes more control over their lives. In 1968, the Kiowa Nation created a governing body called the Kiowa Tribal Council. The council represents both individual Kiowa and the tribe as a whole in talks with the federal government. Areas of concern are health, education, and economic growth.

The chief held the highest position in every band of Kiowa. Band chiefs met to discuss matters that affected the entire tribe.

Economy

Before they met white traders, Kiowa hunters traded with other tribes. The Kiowa traded horses and mules for the vegetables of farming tribes on the Missouri River. They also traded pemmican, which was dried buffalo meat mixed with fat and berries. Later, they traded buffalo hides for European goods. What the Kiowa could not get from trade, they took in raids. They often led raids to steal horses, food, and captives.

On the reservation, government agents tried to turn the Kiowa into farmers. Kiowa hunter-warriors looked down on farming as women's work. They were against the government's plan to break up their land into small plots. They refused to farm. When the buffalo were gone by the 1870s, poverty and a lack of food became common. Within a short time, the Kiowa came to depend on government handouts.

Despite their conflict-filled history with the U.S. government, some Kiowa chose to serve in the U.S. military in World Wars I and II.

Those Kiowa who ran farms did not do well. In the 1930s, they were hurt by the lack of rain and dust storms that hit the Great Plains. Some Kiowa men left to serve in the military in World War I (1914–1918) and World War II (1939–1945).

In the 1950s and 1960s, the U.S. government gave money to young Indians in rural towns if they moved to cities and learned new skills. Many Kiowa moved to Texas and California, where they took jobs as carpenters and laborers. Some stayed behind and leased their land to whites. Still, most Kiowa are very poor. Some earn a little money from the sale of their arts and crafts products.

DAILY LIFE

Education

The Kiowa did not like the U.S. government's attempts to force a white American-style education on their children. They began to distrust white authorities. The tribe's lack of trust led to educational problems that still exist. Over the years, the lack of education led to a gradual loss of the Kiowa language and culture. Over the past fifty years, work has been done to fix the problem. Today, young people are taught the Kiowan language at the Kiowa Tribal Complex in Carnegie, Oklahoma. Many attempts have been made to save Kiowa art, dance, song, and literature. The Kiowa Nation Culture Museum is a center for Kiowa heritage.

The U.S. government made Kiowa children attend schools like this one to get American-style educations.

Tepees provided Kiowa families with shelter and were easy to move.

Tepees

Like other tribes that wandered the Plains, the Kiowa lived in tepees. Wooden poles were set into the ground in the shape of a cone and tied at the top. Buffalo hides were sewn together to cover the poles. The entrance was small, only three or four feet high. It always faced east. The size of a tepee depended on how many people lived in it. Most tepees were home to a family of four or five people. Some tepees were twenty feet wide and at least twenty feet high. Outside, Kiowa tepees were painted with the special symbol of the family who lived there. Some warriors decorated their tepees with the symbol that was painted on their shields.

The inside of the tepee was very plain. In the center was a fire hole to cook food and add warmth. Beds were made from a small frame of willow rods and covered with buffalo skin. They were placed along the edge of the tent. It was the women's job to set up the tepees. The tepees could be set up or broken down quickly as the tribe followed the roaming buffalo herds.

Medicine lodges

The Kiowa came together each spring for the Sun Dance. They built a special building called a medicine lodge. Seventeen poles were set in the ground in a large circle. More poles were placed across their tops to make a roof. Inside, the sacred Sun Dance fetish hung from the center of this frame. Called the *tai-me*, it was a small human figure carved from green stone. The outside of the lodge was covered with cottonwood branches to make walls. The roof was left open to the sky.

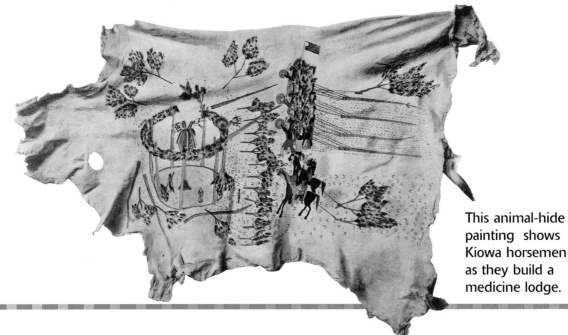

This animal-hide painting shows Kiowa horsemen as they build a medicine lodge.

The Kiowa wore clothing made out of animal hides, which they decorated with fur and beads.

Food

The Kiowa needed the buffalo for food, clothing, and shelter. Kiowa men also killed other large animals, such as antelope, deer, and elk. Women gathered fruits, nuts, and roots to add to the tribe's diet.

Clothing

The Kiowa used animal skins to make most of their clothing. They used the hides of buffalo, deer, and other smaller animals that roamed the Plains. Men wore leggings and buckskin moccasins in the summer months. In the winter, they added a deerskin shirt or a buffalo hide robe. Women wore dresses made of animal skins, along with leggings and moccasins.

The Kiowa adorned themselves with shells, animal bones or teeth, or porcupine quills. Robes were often painted or decorated with embroidery. Animal furs were sometimes worn for warmth. Often, these hides were worn with the animal's head still attached. Warriors used shields painted with figures they saw in dream visions.

Healing practices

The Kiowa believed that animals and other things in nature had spiritual powers. These powers could be used to heal, bring rain, or see the future. Objects such as animal teeth, stones, and food were put in bundles called personal "medicine." This medicine belonged to the shaman (pronounced *SHAH-mun* or *SHAY-mun*). He healed the sick.

The Kiowa believed medicine bundles like this one had healing powers.

Kiowa shamans belonged to the religious society of Buffalo Doctors. They were greatly respected by the other members of the tribe. Buffalo Doctors were given their healing powers in a dream vision. When a Buffalo Doctor healed a sick person, he was richly rewarded.

Arts

Kiowa men and women were famous for their paintings. They used ground-up rocks and soil to make their paints. Men covered their tepees with paintings about their lives and their honors in battle.

Most of the honor and glory in the tribe went to warriors and horse raiders. It was often difficult for a woman to shine. Some Kiowa women belonged to artist societies. Members knew all the secrets of quillwork and beadwork. They would share their secrets for fee. Robes decorated with porcupine quills was highly prized. One of these robes could be traded for a horse.

Kiowa women displayed their artistic talents in quillwork and beadwork designs.

CUSTOMS

Sun Dance

The Sun Dance was held each year in the spring or early summer. Dancers worshiped the Sun and prayed for the rebirth of the buffalo. The ten-day ceremony ended with raids and warfare.

War rituals

The Kiowa held many events to show their bravery and strength. Kiowa warriors gained honor through acts of courage. These acts might be successful in

Members of a Kiowa warrior society, like those pictured here, are honored through dance and sacred rituals.

The warrior enjoyed a social position that was higher than that of most other members of the tribe.

the hunt or "counting coup." This act meant a warrior rode close enough in battle to touch but not kill an enemy. Warrior societies were formed based on age and experience. Young boys were members of the Polanyup, or Rabbit Society.

The highest military honor a man could gain was to be named one of the Koitsenko. They were the greatest and bravest of the Kiowa warriors. There could never be more than ten at one time.

Rank in society

Social rank was clearly marked in Kiowa society. At the top were the *onde*. This group was made up of the finest warriors, leaders, and priests. Beneath them were the *ondegup'a*. This

group included warriors with less wealth and stature. The *kaan* and *dapone*, or poor people, made up most of the tribe.

In this military culture, women were seen as less important than men. They were given most of the household tasks in Kiowa society. They built tepees, cooked food, tanned hides, and made clothing.

Social organizations

In addition to warrior societies, there were religious societies and healing societies such as the Buffalo Doctors and the Owl Doctor Society. Members of the Owl Doctor Society claimed to see into the future. Members of the Eagle Shield Society guarded the tribe's magical and sacred objects.

Sweat baths

One of the most important Kiowa customs was ritual cleansing. It was often the first step in a religious ceremony. It was also a good way to fight illness. The Kiowa entered a sweat lodge to be cleansed. The wooden lodge had a fire that heated rocks and made steam vapor from a nearby water container.

Important events of Kiowa life were pictured on calendars painted on buffalo hide or buckskin.

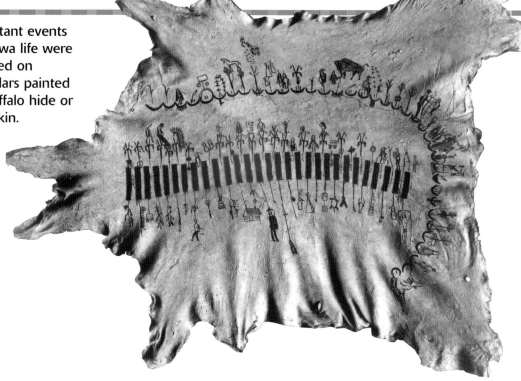

The Kiowa calendar

The Kiowa believed in the importance of a calendar history. Twice each year, the events of the past season were painted on buffalo hides.

Current tribal issues

Today, many of the tribe's problems are the result of their forced move onto the Oklahoma reservation. They live in rural areas far from towns. Many do not have jobs. Health care is poor. Sometimes, the people do not trust government medical centers. The schools often fail to interest Kiowa children or prepare them for future jobs.

This hospital in Oklahoma provides medical services for Native Americans. Some Kiowa, however, are distrustful of medical centers run by the U.S. government.

Notable people

N. Scott Momaday (1934–) is of Kiowa, white, and Cherokee ancestry. He is the Pulitzer Prize–winning author of *House Made of Dawn* (1968). It is the tragic story of a Kiowa man whose life falls apart when he tries to live in a city.

Satanta (1830–1878) was born on the northern Plains. He later moved to the southern Plains with his people. Most of Satanta's adult life was spent in battles against white settlers and the U.S. Army. In 1866, Satanta signed a peace treaty that forced the Kiowa to move onto a

N. Scott Momaday won the Pulitzer Prize for his novel about a Kiowa man's struggles

Satanta dedicated his life to the Kiowa struggle to resist white settlers and the U.S. government.

Kicking Bird, a tribal leader, is just one of many well-known Kiowa.

reservation in present-day Oklahoma. Shortly thereafter, he was taken hostage by U.S. officials. After his release, Satanta led raids against whites in Texas. Satanta was arrested again. He was ordered to stay on the Kiowa reservation. Battles between Indians and whites on the Plains continued. In 1874, Satanta gave himself up to U.S. officials to prove that he was not part of these fights. He was imprisoned anyway, and he died in prison four years later.

Other notable Kiowa include Kiowa/Delaware playwright, editor, and choreographer Hanay

Geiogamah (1945–); tribal leader Kicking Bird (c. 1835–1875); attorney and educator Kirke Kickingbird (1944–); and physician and educator Everett Ronald Rhoades (1931–).

For more information

Brown, Dee. *The War to Save the Buffalo, in Bury My Heart at Wounded Knee.* New York: Henry Holt, 1970.

Haseloff, Cynthia. *The Kiowa Verdict.* Unity, ME: Five Star, 1996.

Wunder, John R. *The Kiowa.* New York: Chelsea House, 1989.

Glossary

Ghost Dance a religion that promised Native Americans a return to their old way of life

Pemmican dried buffalo meat mixed with fat and berries

Peyote a drug made from cactus that was used in some Native American religious ceremonies

Reservation land set aside for Native Americans by the government

Shaman a Native American priest who used magic to heal people and see the future

Sun Dance a ten-day ceremony held each spring to worship the sun

Tepee a tent used as a home by Native Americans

Treaty an agreement between two or more parties

Index